Original title:
Bonding Beyond Barriers

Copyright © 2024 Swan Charm
All rights reserved.

Author: Sara Säde
ISBN HARDBACK: 978-9916-86-560-6
ISBN PAPERBACK: 978-9916-86-561-3
ISBN EBOOK: 978-9916-86-562-0

Harmony in Dissonance

In shadows deep, the whispers rise,
Where chaos breathes, a chance to surmise.
Dissonance brings a strange delight,
A symphony found in the darkest night.

Melodies clash, yet hearts entwine,
In every note, a truth we find.
A tapestry weaves with thread of pain,
In fractured beauty, we still remain.

Colors of Acceptance

A canvas waits, with hues so bright,
Each stroke a story, a path to light.
From every shade, a lesson learned,
In the blend, a fire burned.

The reds of passion, blue's calm embrace,
Together they dance, a vibrant space.
In every color, we find our voice,
In harmony, we make a choice.

Chords of Compassion

In gentle strums, our hearts will meet,
Every chord sings of love's sweet heat.
Compassion flows like a river wide,
A bridge of trust, where we confide.

Through harmonies soft, we rise and fall,
With every note, we hear the call.
Together we stand, hand in hand,
In this music, our spirits expand.

Walking the Same Path

Two pairs of shoes on a winding trail,
With every step, our stories unveil.
Through thorns and blooms, we choose to roam,
In shared laughter, we find our home.

The sun will set, but stars will guide,
In shadowed places, we'll still abide.
Together we walk, our feet in sync,
In every pause, our souls will think.

Crystals of Clarity

In the light, they shimmer bright,
Guiding hearts through the night.
Each facet tells a story true,
A glimpse of hope, a vision new.

Quiet whispers in the air,
Remind us that we must care.
To gaze within, to seek the peace,
Where worries dwindle and fears cease.

Fragments scattered on the ground,
In their beauty, wisdom found.
They reflect the sun's warm glow,
Mapping paths we long to know.

Through the chaos, find the ray,
That leads us gently on our way.
In each crystal, a world unfolds,
A treasure trove of dreams untold.

Holding clarity, we trust the signs,
As life unfolds in sacred lines.
With every step, our spirits rise,
Unraveling the hidden skies.

Bridges Over Troubled Waters

From shore to shore, we span the gap,
With every heartbeat, feel the map.
Underneath the raging tide,
A promise holds, a hope inside.

With every step, a weight gets lighter,
Through turbulent waves, we grow brighter.
When storms arise and nights grow long,
Together, we'll find where we belong.

Each bridge we build, a bond we make,
In the face of fear, we won't forsake.
With hands held tight and dreams aligned,
The strength within will help us find.

As waters rise and shadows loom,
We'll navigate through every gloom.
With trust as our foundation's stone,
We'll venture forth, no longer alone.

Together we rise, as one we stand,
In unity, we make a band.
Through every trial, we will endure,
For love will always find a cure.

The Unfolding Map

In corners worn, secrets hide,
In lines and paths, we will confide.
A journey starts with a single mark,
Leading souls through light and dark.

Each place we visit holds a tale,
Adventures waiting to unveil.
With every twist, a vision grows,
The unfolding map of what life shows.

From mountains high to valleys low,
In every step, new wonders flow.
The compass spins, our futures weave,
In every turn, we learn to believe.

Drawn to the edges of the known,
Seeking truths we can call our own.
With every breath, the path transforms,
Guiding hearts through sun and storms.

Adventure calls, the map extended,
Where dreams are chased, and hopes are blended.
With open minds and souls aglow,
We'll follow where the wild winds blow.

Embracing the Unknown

In shadows cast, we find the light,
Where possibilities take flight.
A leap of faith, a bated breath,
Embracing life, defying death.

With open arms, we greet the gray,
Expecting magic on the way.
From silent fears to joys profound,
In uncertain fields, hope is found.

In every question, treasure lies,
Beneath the surface, beauty sighs.
With every choice, new worlds arise,
In the simple act, wisdom flies.

Each step we take, a dance of chance,
In the unknown, we find our stance.
With courage burning in our chest,
We journey forth, forever blessed.

With eyes wide open, hearts in tow,
We'll pave the path where few dare go.
In the wild unknown, we make our home,
Where dreams of all kind freely roam.

The Warmth of Understanding

In quiet tones, we share our thoughts,
A gentle breeze that soothes the heart.
With every whisper, walls dissolve,
And in that space, new hopes revolve.

Eyes that meet, a spark ignites,
Revealing truths in soft twilight.
The warmth that binds, it softly glows,
In this embrace, our spirits grow.

Through storms we face, we find our way,
With hands held tight, we stay and sway.
The laughter shared, the tears we shed,
In this connection, no words need said.

Each challenge faced, we rise anew,
With open hearts, we journey through.
A tapestry of minds entwined,
In understanding, love we find.

The world outside can fade away,
For here, in trust, we choose to stay.
Together strong, we'll walk the line,
In warmth of understanding, hearts align.

Tides of Togetherness

Like waves that kiss the sandy shore,
We ebb and flow, forever more.
In perfect rhythm, we align,
Each moment shared, a sign divine.

Our laughter echoes through the night,
A beacon shining, pure delight.
In every glance, a story spun,
Two souls entwined, forever one.

With open arms, we face the tide,
Side by side, our hearts our guide.
Through changing seas, we hold on tight,
In togetherness, we find our light.

The storms may come, and winds may roar,
But stronger still, we'll reach the door.
A bond unbroken, deep and vast,
In unity, we free the past.

As time moves on, we'll chart our course,
With love as our unyielding force.
Through every wave, our spirits rise,
In tides of togetherness, we thrive.

The Canvas of Us

With every stroke, our stories blend,
A masterpiece that knows no end.
In vibrant colors, dreams take flight,
Creating joy from darkest nights.

Each brush a touch, each line a trace,
Of laughter's echo, time and space.
The canvas wide, our hearts lay bare,
In every splash, a love to share.

Together we paint the world anew,
With shades of hope and skies so blue.
In tender hues, our lives combine,
A wondrous art, forever shine.

With palettes bright and visions clear,
We paint our truth, we cast our fear.
In every layer, depth and trust,
A canvas formed by love's own rust.

As colors swirl and blend in light,
With every dawn, we seek what's bright.
In the canvas of us, we find our way,
A work of art that will not fray.

Finding Common Ground

In hearts of many, seeds are sown,
A shared desire for love to own.
Through open paths, we look around,
In every smile, there's common ground.

With listening ears and open minds,
In every moment, connection binds.
Together we weave a legacy,
In threads of hope, we choose to be.

Our differences, a colorful array,
In harmony, we find the way.
With hands outstretched, we bridge the void,
In unity, we are employed.

With every step, we walk as one,
With every challenge, we have won.
For in the struggle, we have found,
The beauty of our common ground.

So let us gather, hearts unite,
In understanding, we'll ignite.
Through peace and love, we sow the seed,
In finding common ground, we lead.

When Differences Embrace

When colors blend and hearts unite,
Differences shimmer, a beautiful sight.
Voices rise, a harmonious song,
In this tapestry, we all belong.

With laughter shared and tears overlooked,
Every story adds to the book.
When love transcends the seams that bind,
A greater truth is what we find.

Every culture, a world to explore,
In every clash, we learn to soar.
Respect and trust, the pillars we build,
In embracing differences, our hearts are filled.

So let us gather, hand in hand,
Learning from each, we take a stand.
Together we rise, together we dance,
In our diversity, there lies a chance.

Together Under One Sky

Beneath the vast and starry dome,
We share the earth, we share our home.
Each heart beats with a different tune,
Yet, together we look at the moon.

Amidst the chaos, peace we seek,
Finding strength in every weak.
With open arms and open minds,
A unity of varied kinds.

Through every storm, we stand as one,
Fighting for a brighter sun.
Together we rise, we break the chain,
Finding joy amidst the pain.

In whispered words, our hopes align,
Drawing closer, your hand in mine.
Under the same sky, dreams ignite,
Together, we shine, our spirits bright.

Journey of Shared Stories

Every tale spun, a thread in time,
Whispers of hope in prose and rhyme.
Through pages worn and hearts aglow,
Together we learn, together we grow.

From distant lands, we gather here,
Voices echo, loud and clear.
Every chapter holds a spark,
Illuminating paths, lighting the dark.

Our histories woven, rich and deep,
In memories treasured, the stories we keep.
With every sigh, with every cheer,
Shared tales bind us, year after year.

In laughter and sorrow, we find our place,
In stories told, we embrace grace.
Together we voyage, hand in hand,
Writing our saga, a united band.

Threads of Connection

Invisible strings weave our lives,
Binding hearts where kindness thrives.
Through every challenge, we stand tall,
With threads of love, we won't let fall.

In every smile, in every tear,
These threads of connection draw us near.
A tapestry rich with vibrant hues,
In our union, we cannot lose.

We share the burdens, the weight we share,
In every struggle, we show we care.
Together we laugh, together we weep,
With threads of connection, our bonds run deep.

So let us cherish and nurture this art,
In every gesture, the love we impart.
In the fabric of life, forever we'll stay,
Woven together, come what may.

Meeting at the Crossroads

Two paths meet, in whispered light,
Choices linger, day and night.
Footsteps echo on laden ground,
Silent promises all around.

In the twilight, shadows blend,
A moment's pause, a chance to mend.
Eyes connect with fleeting grace,
Paths converge in a sacred space.

Voices murmur, tales unfold,
Stories shared, both brave and bold.
In the balance, futures sway,
Meeting here, we choose our way.

Underneath the stars so bright,
Dreams take flight in shared insight.
Together we stand, strong and free,
At the crossroads, just you and me.

This crossing holds a magic rare,
In unity, we've found our care.
With every step, new paths refine,
Meeting here, our hearts entwine.

Where Hearts Converge

In quiet corners, dreams are spun,
Where hearts converge, and hope's begun.
Hands reach out in gentle plea,
Together crafting destiny.

Through every tear, laughter shines,
Binding souls with tender lines.
Each moment holds a spark of light,
Illuminating the darkest night.

In unison, we hum a song,
In this dance, we both belong.
Every heartbeat echoes clear,
A symphony for us to hear.

With open arms, we bridge the space,
Where love resides, a warm embrace.
In every corner, truth emerges,
Here in this place, where hearts converge.

Together walking, hand in hand,
Finding footing on this land.
In every glance, a tale we weave,
Where hearts converge, we dare believe.

Uniting the Distant

Miles apart, yet close in heart,
Uniting the distant, we play our part.
Thoughts like bridges span the night,
In dreams, we hold our shared light.

Voices carried on the breeze,
Messages sent with gentle ease.
Across the space, our spirits meet,
In every word, a rhythmic beat.

The universe feels our embrace,
Uniting souls in sacred space.
Each connection sparks a fire,
Igniting in us a shared desire.

When shadows creep and doubts arise,
We find the strength in shared skies.
Together, though we stand apart,
Uniting the distant, heart to heart.

In every sunset, every dawn,
A tapestry of love is drawn.
Through time and space, we intertwine,
In the distance, our hearts align.

Threads of Understanding

Woven softly, threads align,
In a world where hearts entwine.
With every stitch, a story told,
Threads of understanding, brave and bold.

In colors bright and patterns clear,
Together, we chase away the fear.
Each conversation, a thread anew,
Binding us closer, me and you.

Through laughter shared and burdens borne,
Our tapestry is gently worn.
In every challenge, a chance to grow,
Threads of understanding begin to flow.

With guiding hands, we mend the frays,
Crafting moments through our days.
Each knot tied with care and grace,
Threads of understanding find their place.

In the fabric of life, we stand,
Together weaving dreams so grand.
Through time and trials, we shall see,
Threads of understanding set us free.

Strands of Trust

In whispers shared, we weave our ties,
A gentle dance beneath the skies.
Each promise flows like rivers deep,
A bond nurtured, ours to keep.

Through storms and trials, hand in hand,
Together, we will make our stand.
In honesty, we find our way,
A light that guides us day by day.

When shadows fall, and doubts arise,
We lift each other, hearts the prize.
With every laugh, each tear we shed,
Our trust, a tapestry that's spread.

So let us cherish what we build,
A world of faith, our dreams fulfilled.
In every moment, gift of grace,
Strands of trust, our sacred space.

A Symphony of Lives

In every heart, a note unique,
Together sung, the harmony speaks.
Diverse our paths, but intertwined,
A melody of souls aligned.

Through rhythms shared, we find our way,
In laughter's joy, in sorrow's sway.
Each voice a thread, together blend,
Creating beauty without end.

When storms arise and tempests roar,
We rise united, hearts explore.
In every chord, a story told,
Of dreams and hopes, of love so bold.

With passions fierce, we dance through strife,
Transforming pain into new life.
A symphony that knows no cease,
In unity, we find our peace.

Together, We Rise

When darkness falls, we light the way,
Our spirits fierce, we will not sway.
In silent strength, we stand as one,
Together, battles fought and won.

Each challenge faced, a chance to grow,
In shared resolve, our courage shows.
From valleys low to mountains high,
With every heartbeat, we will fly.

In laughter's song or sorrow's night,
We lift each other, hold on tight.
With arms entwined, we find our place,
Together, we embrace the grace.

Though storms may come, we will not yield,
In unity, our hearts are healed.
Together, we face the world anew,
A tapestry of hope in view.

The Beauty of Differences

In shades of skin and heart's embrace,
A world adorned with every face.
Our stories rich, like colors blend,
In differences, true beauty sends.

Each voice a note in life's broad song,
Together, where we all belong.
In varying dreams and cultures wide,
We find the strength that is our pride.

With open hearts, we share our space,
In every smile, a warm embrace.
The beauty lies in all we are,
Bright constellations, each a star.

In understanding, we transcend,
Through every hand that we extend.
Together, we find our way to see,
The beauty of all humanity.

Threads that Tie Us

In shadows cast by golden day,
We stitch our dreams in soft array.
With every breath, a bond we weave,
In every heart, the threads believe.

Through laughter shared and tears that flow,
These threads connect, they gently grow.
A tapestry of moments bright,
Together we rise, with love as light.

Across the miles, they hold us near,
In whispered hopes, we feel no fear.
Though storms may rage and time erode,
Our hearts bound tight, shared love our code.

So when the night feels cold and long,
Remember this: our love is strong.
Each thread a tale, a journey's mark,
Together we'll shine, ignite the dark.

In hands entwined, we'll face the dawn,
Forever tied, we journey on.
These threads of love, a sacred trust,
In every heartbeat, hope is thrust.

Hearts Entwined

In quiet whispers, hearts align,
Two souls entwined, a love divine.
Through storms we dance, through light we glide,
With every step, you're by my side.

In gentle moments, silent glee,
Our hearts beat soft, a symphony.
With fingers clasped, we share the dream,
In every glance, a lover's theme.

Against the tide, we stand as one,
In shadows cast by setting sun.
Together we rise, defy the night,
Your heart, my compass, leads to light.

Through tangled paths, we find our way,
In laughter bright, we seize the day.
With every tear, a lesson learned,
In love's embrace, our passion burned.

So let the world around us fade,
In our small bubble, love won't shade.
Hearts intertwined, we are complete,
With every beat, our souls repeat.

Borders of the Heart

Across the lines, where worlds collide,
In every glance, our hopes abide.
With whispered dreams in moonlit air,
We find a place to call our share.

In shades of dusk, our spirits merge,
A river's flow, a gentle surge.
No borders drawn can keep us far,
In love's embrace, you are my star.

With every laugh, we break the mold,
In stories shared, our hearts unfold.
Together we stand, a fearless pair,
In every sigh, a silent prayer.

Through stormy nights and sunny days,
In every twist, love finds its ways.
No walls can hold what hearts express,
In love's vast sea, we find our rest.

So let the maps map out their claim,
Our hearts will forge a different flame.
With every pulse, we venture new,
No borders hold what love can do.

Fireflies in the Fog

In twilight's glow, where shadows play,
Fireflies dance in soft decay.
They weave through mist, a fleeting sight,
Guiding lost souls to warm the night.

With every flicker, a whisper soft,
They catch the dreams that soar aloft.
In soft embrace, the darkness yields,
As light reveals what sorrow shields.

Through fields of green, they twirl and sway,
Reminding hearts to find their way.
In gentle spark, the hope ignites,
As fireflies beckon with vibrant lights.

In every heart, they leave a trace,
A promise made to hold our place.
When fog descends and covers wide,
Their glow invites us to confide.

So let us dance beneath the stars,
With fireflies, we'll heal our scars.
In secret realms where magic lies,
We find our peace, beneath the skies.

Embracing Differences

In every laugh, a story told,
In every heart, a dream unfolds.
Colors blend in vibrant light,
Together we shine, day and night.

Voices echo, strong and clear,
Different paths, yet we draw near.
Through our trials, we will grow,
Hand in hand, together we sow.

Like petals in a blooming flower,
We find strength in every hour.
Each skin tone, a brilliant hue,
United in the shades we brew.

Songs of joy, we harmonize,
In our differences, brilliance lies.
With open hearts and minds that dare,
We'll build a world that's bold and rare.

So let us dance, both wise and free,
Embracing all, just you and me.
As we weave our stories tight,
In unity, we'll find our light.

Unseen Hands Unite

Across the miles, unseen they reach,
In silent whispers, they beseech.
Holding dreams with gentle care,
These unseen hands, always there.

Through every struggle, pain, and fear,
A bond unbreakable draws near.
Finding solace in the night,
We stand together, hearts alight.

In quiet moments, strength is found,
A heartbeat shared, a sacred sound.
Though apart, we feel the tie,
Invisible threads that never die.

When shadows fall and hope is thin,
We rise again, we always win.
These hands unite from far and wide,
In a tapestry, we confide.

Together we dream, together we stand,
Unseen but felt, a guiding hand.
With faith in love, we'll find our way,
Through every night into the day.

The Tapestry of Togetherness

Each thread a tale, each hue a sound,
In this tapestry, we are bound.
Woven tightly, hearts entwined,
Strength in numbers, peace defined.

Echoes of laughter, whispers of grace,
In every corner, a friendly face.
Together we rise, together we fall,
A tapestry bright, uniting us all.

The fabric of life, both rich and rare,
Threads of compassion, love, and care.
Each knot a promise, each stitch a vow,
In this woven dream, we find our now.

Colors dance, both fierce and bold,
In unity, a story unfolds.
Through storms and trials, we remain,
In this shared weave, there's no more pain.

So let us cherish this art we share,
In every heartbeat, in every prayer.
Together we'll craft a future bright,
In the tapestry of love and light.

Rivers of Shared Dreams

Flowing gently, dreams align,
In rivers deep, life's design.
Currents pull us close and near,
Waves of hope, we hold so dear.

Each twist and turn, a tale revealed,
In unity, our fate is sealed.
The waters rise, yet we hold fast,
In shared ambitions, we are cast.

From mountains high to valleys low,
These rivers teach us how to grow.
In every drop, a spark ignites,
Together, we soar to new heights.

Let us sail on this gentle stream,
With every heartbeat, live the dream.
Through trials faced and joys embraced,
In shared rivers, our fears are chased.

So journey on, my friend, with me,
In rivers deep and hearts set free.
Together, we'll navigate the bends,
In shared dreams, our story never ends.

Aligning Stars

In the vast expanse, they shine bright,
Whispers of dreams in the night light.
Guiding us softly through the dark,
Each shimmering point, a hopeful spark.

A dance of fate, a cosmic thread,
We reach for wonders, where we are led.
In silence, they twinkle, telling us true,
Together united, as spirits break through.

The universe hums a secret tune,
As planets spin 'neath a silver moon.
With every heartbeat, sync with the flow,
As stars align, our paths will glow.

Wishes are cast on the night's embrace,
While stardust lingers in time and space.
Through trials faced, and battles fought,
Connections forged in the lessons taught.

As constellations form a map unknown,
We find our way, never alone.
The journey ahead, with hearts that dare,
In the realm of dreams, we become aware.

Together on Divergent Paths

Two roads diverge, in different ways,
Yet side by side, we share our days.
With laughter and tears, our stories blend,
In the heart's embrace, we find a friend.

You step ahead, but I will follow,
Through every joy and every hollow.
Our footprints trace, where shadows blend,
In moments held, we will transcend.

The world may twist, and often turn,
But the fire of trust will always burn.
In the silence, our spirits dance,
Holding on tight to every chance.

Seasons change, yet we remain,
Through the sunshine and the rain.
Each journey taken, a tale to tell,
In different ways, we know it well.

Together strong, yet free to roam,
In every heart, we find a home.
Though paths may differ, we'll always share,
The bond between us, beyond compare.

Fellowship of the Unique

In a world so vast, we stand apart,
Each with a gift, a vibrant heart.
Colors of life, in shades diverse,
Together we weave, a universe.

With stories rich, and dreams untold,
In every chapter, new paths unfold.
The beauty lies in differences made,
In unity shared, no need for parade.

Voices rise in harmonious chant,
Though our rhythms and beats may enchant.
Celebrating each twist of fate,
A mosaic of souls, we cultivate.

In laughter's echo, and in our sighs,
Across every tear, our spirit flies.
A fellowship blooms, unlike any other,
In the garden of life, we each are a flower.

So let us gather, hand in hand,
In the warmth of acceptance, we stand.
Together we shine, distinct yet near,
In fellowship true, we conquer our fear.

We All Belong

In the tapestry of life, threads entwine,
Each unique pattern a sacred sign.
A space for everyone, hearts open wide,
In the circle of souls, we may confide.

With arms outstretched, we welcome grace,
Each voice matters in this vast space.
From whispers soft to shouts of cheer,
In every story, we hold dear.

No shadows cast when the light is shared,
Together for justice, we'll be prepared.
Infinite colors, a vibrant song,
In unity's strength, we all belong.

Through trials faced and victories won,
Together we rise, as one we run.
Fulfilling the promise of days to come,
In each heartbeat, our anthem hums.

So let love guide the journeys we take,
With open arms, let the barriers break.
Hand in hand, let's take this stand,
In the hall of hearts, we understand.

Unity in Diversity

In every color, every face,
A tapestry of human grace.
Different paths, yet side by side,
Together in this great wide ride.

Languages spoken, stories shared,
Hearts entwined, we are prepared.
Our roots may differ in the ground,
But in our strength, we are found.

Hand in hand, we start to dance,
A world united, not by chance.
Celebrate what makes us whole,
In our diversity, we find the soul.

Through winding roads, we learn to grow,
With open minds, our spirits glow.
Each voice matters, come take part,
For unity begins in the heart.

Together we rise, together we stand,
Weaving connection across our land.
In unity's embrace, we thrive,
In our togetherness, we come alive.

Tides of Empathy

Like waves upon the sandy shore,
Empathy flows, forevermore.
With every tide, we learn and feel,
A shared connection, deep and real.

The rhythm of hearts, the pull of the sea,
In times of struggle, we find unity.
With open arms, we bridge the gap,
Waking in kindness from the world's nap.

Through ebb and flow, we seek the light,
In understanding, we find our sight.
A gentle nudge, a heartfelt song,
With every gesture, we grow strong.

In moments fleeting, we leave our mark,
A spark of love ignites the dark.
Let currents guide us to a place,
Where empathy warms with its embrace.

Together we rise, wave after wave,
Holding each other, brave and brave.
For in this dance, we find our grace,
In tides of empathy, we embrace.

Voices in the Wind

Whispers carried by the breeze,
Stories shared among the trees.
Voices mingling, soft and clear,
A chorus found, inviting near.

Each note a dream, each sound a song,
In the quiet, we all belong.
The wind carries truths from far and wide,
Gifts of wisdom bound to guide.

We listen close to tales untold,
In every heart, a warmth we hold.
Messages drift, and we must heed,
The call of love, in thought and deed.

In the rustling leaves, we find our way,
Voices harmonize, night and day.
Together we rise, as spirits blend,
In the wind's embrace, we transcend.

So let us sing with all our might,
In the winds of change, we find our light.
A symphony of souls set free,
Voices in the wind, a melody.

Windows of Opportunity

Glimmers of hope in every dawn,
Through windows wide, a new day's drawn.
Each moment a chance to take a leap,
In every heartbeat, dreams we keep.

Open the shutters, let the light in,
Discover the joy that lies within.
Each chance we seize, a step we climb,
In every risk, a dance with time.

With courage fierce, we face the call,
For opportunities come to all.
A chance encounter, a spark ignites,
Windows open to wondrous sights.

Through paths unknown and skies so vast,
Embrace the moment; hold it fast.
With open hearts, we find our way,
In windows of chance, we seize the day.

So scatter your fears, let dreams expand,
For life awaits, just take a hand.
In every window, futures gleam,
Together we weave our greatest dream.

Whispers Across the Divide

In shadows soft, a voice will sigh,
A gentle breeze from far away.
It carries tales, of love and loss,
Across the night, in soft array.

With every star that twinkles bright,
A secret shared, a truth unveiled.
The hearts in silence softly speak,
In whispers sweet, where hope has sailed.

From distant shores, a call we hear,
It binds the souls that long to meet.
In voices shared, we find our way,
In every note, our hearts complete.

When bridges fall and gaps divide,
We find a path, though far apart.
In gentle words, they bridge the night,
In steadfast love, we share our heart.

So lift your voice, let echoes play,
In harmony, we rise above.
For every whisper, every sigh,
Brings us together, bound by love.

Flowers Blooming in the Cracks

Amidst the stone, a life will rise,
A burst of color in the gray.
It fights for light against the odds,
In cracks where shadows used to play.

With petals bright, it greets the sun,
Defiant blooms in harsh terrain.
They sway in rhythm with the breeze,
A testament to hope's refrain.

Each fragile stem tells tales of strength,
Of battles fought, of dreams held tight.
In every bloom, a story grows,
Of resilience in the night.

Though burdens bear, they stand in grace,
Their beauty shines through broken ground.
In every fragrance, joy reborn,
From what was lost, new life is found.

So let us learn from blooms that thrive,
In places where we least expect.
For even when the world seems harsh,
Hope finds a way, our hearts connect.

The Language of Kindness

In softest tones, we share our hearts,
A gentle touch, a warm embrace.
With every word, we weave a thread,
Connecting souls in quiet space.

A smile exchanged, a moment shared,
In gestures small, love finds its way.
The language of kindness speaks so clear,
In notes of care, it holds its sway.

No need for words to cast a spell,
For kindness blooms with every act.
It holds the power to uplift,
To mend the wounds where hope is cracked.

It thrives in warmth, in patience shown,
In listening hearts, as dreams take flight.
For kindness calls in every form,
A beacon glowing through the night.

So let us speak in love today,
In every glance, and every smile.
For kindness is a universal tongue,
That makes the distance so worthwhile.

More Than Meets the Eye

Beneath the surface, depths await,
Where stories hide and dreams reside.
In every glance, a world unfolds,
A tapestry of truth and pride.

The quiet moments, soft and still,
Reveal the hearts we seek to know.
In whispered thoughts and silent sighs,
The beauty lies in what we show.

For every smile holds deeper hopes,
And laughter masks a hidden pain.
In shadows cast, the light shall dance,
In every storm, a chance to gain.

So look beyond the surface bright,
For wisdom dwells in layers deep.
In every soul, a story flows,
In every heart, the dreams we keep.

With open eyes and open hearts,
We find our way through dark and light.
For life's a canvas, bold and wide,
Where more than meets the eye ignites.

Connections in the Silence

In quiet moments shared with breath,
A gentle peace glides overhead.
Thoughts intertwine in whispers soft,
Bound by the love we both bequeath.

Though words may fail, our hearts endure,
Each glance a story, rich and pure.
Through unspoken ties we understand,
In silence, we find our truth secure.

The space between speaks volumes loud,
In every heartbeat, we are proud.
A tapestry of hopes and dreams,
In the stillness, we are vowed.

A language formed in gentle sighs,
Where laughter dances and never dies.
In moments lost and times we've missed,
Our souls connect, where silence lies.

So let us linger in this space,
Where every thought finds its place.
In bonds unseen, we light the day,
In silence, love leaves no trace.

Unity of the Uncommon

In a world where differences bloom,
We gather light to dispel the gloom.
Each voice a note in vibrant song,
Together we find a way to loom.

Strange paths we tread, yet side by side,
In every heart, a spark to guide.
Embracing shadows, chasing light,
Our strength in unity, we abide.

The colors blend, a canvas bright,
A vivid clash, yet pure delight.
In every struggle, hands we share,
Creating harmony from the fight.

Uncommon tales that weave and twine,
Each story rich, a glistening vine.
As we walk together, hearts entwined,
In diverse beauty, love will shine.

So let our differences unite,
A world of wonder, bold and bright.
In every moment, let us show
The unity found in the twilight.

Weaving Together

Threads of color in hands so skilled,
We spin a fabric, dreams fulfilled.
With every stitch a tale untold,
In warmth and comfort, hearts are thrilled.

Each pattern tells of joy and strife,
A shared connection, woven life.
In delicate balance, we create,
A masterpiece of love and light.

With every knot, a memory binds,
In laughter's echo, soft reminders find.
We gather fragments, hopes and fears,
Together forging, hearts entwined.

As we work, our spirits grow,
In every thread, our passion flows.
With purpose clear, we breathe and live,
In weaving time, our essence shows.

So let us craft with hands of grace,
To share this world, our sacred space.
In unity, we will remain,
As we weave together, face to face.

Beyond the Divide

Over mountains high and rivers wide,
Where echoes linger, worlds collide.
In every heart, the longing stirs,
To bridge the gap, our souls allied.

Within the silence, a whisper calls,
Through every barrier, love installs.
Beyond the walls that separate,
A thread of hope that never falls.

In shadows deep where doubts may fade,
We gather courage unafraid.
To seek the light that softly glows,
In every choice, foundations laid.

Through storms that rage and tears that flow,
Compassion's light begins to show.
In unity, we find the way,
Beyond the divide, our spirits grow.

So hand in hand, we cross the lines,
Embracing all that time defines.
With every step, we dare to dream,
Beyond the divide, our hearts align.

Whispers of Unity

In the quiet of the night, we stand,
Holding hands, seeking light,
Voices soft as the breeze,
Carrying dreams that never cease.

Hearts entwined like vines that grow,
Each whisper a promise to sow,
Through the storms of doubt we tread,
With hope as our steady thread.

Together we face the tides that clash,
With courage found in every clash,
Bound by ties that won't unbind,
In each other, peace we find.

From diverse paths, we find our way,
Stitching fragments day by day,
In unity, a tapestry bright,
Woven with threads of shared light.

The whispers call us to be one,
Underneath the same warm sun,
In our hearts, we hold the key,
To a world of harmony.

The Fabric of Belonging

In a world so wide and vast,
We search for roots that hold us fast,
Threads of laughter, threads of tears,
Intertwined through all our years.

Every story forms the loom,
Crafting warmth where shadows loom,
In the colors, bold and bright,
We find our place and shine our light.

With every stitch, a bond is formed,
In hands of strangers, love is warmed,
Together strong, we weave the tape,
Creating dreams that dare escape.

The fabric stretches, yet stays tight,
In diverse paths, we find our sight,
Bound by moments, big and small,
In this embrace, we rise, we fall.

As we gather, near or far,
Each voice a thread, each heart a star,
Together in this quilt of soul,
We find our peace, we feel whole.

Creating New Paths

With each step, we carve the ground,
In the silence, new dreams found,
Worn shoes mark the trails we've made,
In fresh soil, our hopes cascade.

Whispers of change tug at our hearts,
In every ending, new life starts,
Through tangled brambles, we will go,
With courage fierce, and minds aglow.

Each direction is an open door,
To venture forth, to seek for more,
Hands together, we shall create,
A brand new path that feels like fate.

From shadows past, we rise anew,
With visions clear, we break on through,
In every heartbeat, echoes ring,
Together we will boldly sing.

Future beckons with open arms,
In every barrier, find the charms,
Creating trails for those who seek,
A legacy where hope won't leak.

Lighthouses in Fog

In the misty twilight's grasp,
We seek beacons, firm to clasp,
Lighthouses cast their glowing beams,
Guiding us through whispered dreams.

When the waves crash and shadows loom,
We find solace in their bloom,
With every flicker, hope ignites,
In darkest hours, love invites.

Waves of doubt may rise and swell,
Yet here they stand, our homes to dwell,
A steady light amidst the haze,
In their glow, our spirits blaze.

Together we face the stormy night,
With lighthouses, our hearts take flight,
In unity, we won't lose our way,
For love's light will always stay.

As dawn breaks, our fears will fade,
With every sunrise, hope is laid,
In every heart, a guide we'll find,
Together, forever intertwined.

Hands Across the Divide

Two souls reach out with grace,
Bridging distances we face.
In silence speaks a heart so true,
Finding solace, me and you.

Winds of change, they softly call,
Together we rise, never fall.
With open hands, we cross the line,
In unity, our spirits shine.

Though paths may twist and turn away,
In this bond, we choose to stay.
Hope ignites a vibrant flame,
In our hearts, we feel the same.

Through stormy skies and calm ahead,
Words unspoken, yet well said.
With laughter shared, we weave a dream,
A tapestry, a gentle gleam.

Together we'll dance, hand in hand,
In this moment, together we stand.
No borders built can ever confine,
For love's embrace is truly divine.

In the Realm of Together

In this realm, we're not alone,
Each voice a melody, a tone.
Diverse threads woven, rich and bold,
A story of warmth, yet untold.

Moments shared, like stars that gleam,
Together we build, together we dream.
Every heartbeat, a sweet refrain,
In unity, we break the chain.

With every step on this shared ground,
New friendships blossom, hope is found.
Hand in hand, we'll light the dark,
In every soul, a vital spark.

Through laughter, tears, we stitch our fate,
In this tapestry, we resonate.
Embracing differences, we find grace,
In every journey, a sacred place.

Together we rise, in harmony's embrace,
A tapestry of love, our sacred space.
In the realm of together, hearts ignite,
Crafting our future, shining bright.

Strength in Differences

In our colors, strength is found,
Different whispers, a vibrant sound.
Like a garden, full of life,
We bloom together, free from strife.

Elevated voices, strong and clear,
In our truths, we dance, we steer.
Threads of culture, rich and bright,
In this quilt, we find our light.

Each unique song adds to the score,
Together, we can soar and soar.
In understanding, we find our way,
Strength in differences leads the day.

Through every challenge, hand in hand,
In unity, we make our stand.
One heart, one hope, we elevate,
In each other's arms, we celebrate.

Diverse paths meeting on one road,
In the journey, love's the code.
Together, we rewrite the old,
In strength, we find our stories told.

Shared Dreams of Tomorrow

In the dawning light, we gather near,
Voices rising, calm and clear.
Our dreams entwined, like vines they grow,
In the heart, a radiant glow.

With every step towards the new,
Hope dances, vibrant and true.
Together we seek, together we strive,
In shared dreams, we come alive.

Lifting each other, hand in hand,
In this journey, we take a stand.
Each vision bright, a guiding star,
In unity, we'll travel far.

Tomorrow calls with open arms,
In our love, we find our charms.
Through every struggle, we shall reap,
The dreams we share, the promises keep.

A world of wonder lies ahead,
In every heart, a dream is fed.
Together we'll build a brighter day,
In shared dreams, we find our way.

Stones Transformed into Bridges

Upon the riverbed they rest,
Silent, steadfast, holding fast.
Through time and tide they bear a quest,
To form a path, together cast.

Where once were barriers, now align,
In reaching out, we learn to bind.
These stones, with purpose, intertwine,
Creating bonds, so kind, so blind.

With every step upon the span,
We leave behind the weight of fear.
For in this journey, hand in hand,
We pave the way, and hold most dear.

Nature's grace in stone we find,
The journey forged in shared embrace.
Our hearts, like bridges, open wide,
Connecting worlds, a sacred space.

Stones once cold, now warm and bright,
Built by the hope of many hands.
Together we can face the night,
Transformed by love where kindness stands.

Merging Souls

In twilight's glow, your hand in mine,
Two spirits dance, both intertwined.
With whispered dreams, our hearts align,
Merging paths, our lives defined.

Through laughter shared and silent tears,
A tapestry of moments blend.
Each secret known, dissolving fears,
Together strong, we do transcend.

In every gaze, a story told,
Reflections deep of love's embrace.
Two souls, once timid, now bold,
In unity, we find our place.

The world outside may shift and change,
Yet here, we stand, a steadfast cheer.
With every heartbeat, life grows strange,
But in your arms, I hold what's clear.

As seasons pass and time moves slow,
We'll cherish every fleeting hour.
In merging worlds, two hearts will glow,
In love, we bloom, our greatest power.

The Universe in Our Eyes

Glimmers of stardust softly shine,
Reflecting worlds both near and far.
In every glance, a truth divine,
We hold the cosmos, like a star.

Through skies of blue and darkest night,
Our dreams take flight, a wondrous drift.
Each heartbeat sings with pure delight,
In every moment, we uplift.

The galaxies swirl in our minds,
An endless dance of love and fate.
With every thought, new worlds we find,
In unity, we resonate.

With every laugh, the heavens sigh,
In silence shared, the cosmos hums.
Together, we can reach the sky,
For in our hearts, the universe comes.

So let us gaze with open eyes,
At wonders wrapped in stardust dreams.
Through love, we see the world's disguise,
For in our souls, the vastness gleams.

Roots Intertwined

Beneath the earth, our roots descend,
Twisting deep in a silent dance.
Through shadows cast, they learn to blend,
In union's hold, they find their chance.

From distant lands, we've come to grow,
Linked by a bond that intertwines.
Through storm and sun, together flow,
In every struggle, love defines.

With whispers shared beneath the soil,
We draw the strength to rise above.
Through trials faced and toil,
Together, we become the love.

Branches reach toward the bright sky,
While roots descend to hold us tight.
Through seasons change, we will not die,
In unity, we find our light.

So let us flourish, hand in hand,
In rich soil where our hearts reside.
For in this life, together stand,
Our roots entwined, our endless guide.

Colors of Connection

In hues of red and gentle blue,
We find our paths, both old and new.
Each shade a voice, a tale to tell,
In colors bright, we weave our spell.

Golden threads of laughter's cheer,
Bind us close, both far and near.
In every glance, a soft embrace,
Together we dance, a vibrant grace.

Emerald green in nature's art,
Whispers of love that fill the heart.
Through every storm, we stand our ground,
In every shade, our strength is found.

With every color, a bond we trace,
In every smile, a sacred space.
Together, we rise, hand in hand,
In this spectrum, forever we stand.

So let us paint the world anew,
With kindness bright, in all we do.
In colors bold, our spirits soar,
A masterpiece that we explore.

Broken Chains

In silent cries, the whispers wake,
A call for freedom, hearts to break.
We rise as one, against the night,
With hopeful dreams that search for light.

The weight of chains, we cast away,
In unity, we find our way.
With voices strong, we pave the path,
Together we stand, defying wrath.

Each lost soul, a story told,
In the fire of hope, we are bold.
For every tear we've ever shed,
Is a step towards the life we've led.

Through valleys deep, the shadows creep,
Yet in our hearts, the light we keep.
Bound no more, we walk as free,
In the strength of love, our destiny.

So let the echoes rise and ring,
In every heart, a song to sing.
With broken chains, we lift our gaze,
Towards the dawn of brighter days.

Open Hearts

In the stillness of the night,
Open hearts can feel the light.
With every pulse, a gentle beat,
A rhythm shared, our souls meet.

In kindness offered, walls come down,
A simple smile, a shared frown.
We weave our dreams with threads of grace,
In open hearts, we find our place.

Through every trial, hand in hand,
Together we stand, united, grand.
With every story, we gather close,
In warmth of hearts, that's where we chose.

With open hearts, we learn to see,
The beauty in diversity.
In every laugh and every tear,
We build a world where all are near.

So let us tend this sacred flame,
In open hearts, we'll share our name.
For love is vast, it knows no end,
In unity, our spirits blend.

Voices of the Many

In the echo of a thousand cries,
The strength of hope begins to rise.
Each voice a note in harmony,
Together we sing, wild and free.

From valleys low to mountains high,
Through storms of change, we learn to fly.
In every heart, a story grows,
The voices of many, peace bestows.

With every word, a bridge we make,
For understanding, for love's own sake.
In unity, we shine so bright,
Guided by the stars at night.

Through whispered dreams and shouts of joy,
In every struggle, we deploy.
For in our differences, we find,
The voices of many, intertwined.

So let the anthem ring so clear,
In every heart, we draw you near.
With voices strong, we'll pave the way,
For brighter tomorrows, come what may.

Beyond the Borders of the Heart

In lands afar, where rivers gleam,
Love knows no boundaries, fuels the dream.
In whispered kindness, we find the way,
Beyond the borders, hearts will sway.

Through mountains tall and oceans wide,
In every soul, our hopes reside.
With open arms, we bridge the gap,
A tapestry of kindness wrapped.

In every tear, a seed is sown,
In every smile, connections grown.
For love can cross the fiercest tide,
Together we stand, side by side.

So let us journey, hand in hand,
To distant shores, to promised land.
In every heart, a flame we start,
Beyond the borders, love's true art.

In every rhythm, a song we share,
Together we'll rise, beyond despair.
In unity's strength, we chart the course,
For beyond the borders, flows love's source.

In the Garden of Souls

In the shades where shadows play,
Whispers weave through leaves and clay.
Silent blooms of every hue,
Dance beneath the skies so blue.

Footsteps trace the path of light,
Guiding dreams through day and night.
Every seed, a story told,
In this garden, brave and bold.

Petals fall like gentle tears,
Carrying the weight of years.
In the stillness, time stands still,
Breath of life, an ancient thrill.

Roots entwined, a sacred bond,
Nature sings, a soothing song.
Love and loss, we meet them here,
In the garden, all is clear.

So lie among the fragrant blooms,
Let your spirit shed like plumes.
In this space, your heart can soar,
In the garden, be restored.

The Power of Composure

In the storm, a steady grace,
Calm resolve, a measured pace.
When the world seems full of fright,
Hold your ground, embrace the light.

Waves may crash, but you stand tall,
Anchor deep, you will not fall.
In the chaos, find your ease,
Breathe in strength, exhale the breeze.

Silence whispers like a friend,
Gentle thoughts that never bend.
In your heart, a fortress grows,
Facing battles, facing foes.

Stillness holds a sacred key,
Unlocking all that you can be.
With composure, rise anew,
Embrace the peace inside of you.

In the depths of trials faced,
Step by step, you'll find your place.
Through the storms, you'll learn to see,
The power lives inside of me.

Welcoming the Unfamiliar

Open doors to worlds unknown,
New horizons, seeds are sown.
In the steps of those who roam,
Find the courage to call home.

Voices echo through the air,
Different tales, each one a prayer.
Hold their stories, allow the flow,
In the mix, new bonds will grow.

Colors swirl in vibrant dance,
Each exchange, a fleeting chance.
Leave your comfort, step outside,
In the novel, take great pride.

Curiosity like a flame,
Burning bright, it shares no shame.
With each touch, each heartfelt glance,
In the unfamiliar, find romance.

Welcoming souls from far and wide,
Together on this wondrous ride.
In the new, find what is dear,
Embrace the rich, both far and near.

From Many, One

We stand together, hand in hand,
Different stories shape this land.
In our hearts, we weave a thread,
From many paths, the common shred.

Voices rise in harmony,
Sing a tune of unity.
Though diverse, our spirits blend,
On this journey, we depend.

Strength in numbers, wisdom shared,
Building bridges, love declared.
Through the fire, through the rain,
From many, strength we gain.

Each experience, a piece of art,
Collective dreams begin to start.
In our differences, we find,
A vibrant quilt that ties the mind.

Together as we light the dawn,
We are many, yet we're one.
In our unity, we feel alive,
From many stories, hope will thrive.

The Tapestry of Us

Threads of laughter weave so tight,
In the fabric of day and night.
Whispers of dreams, gently spun,
Together we rise, as one.

Colorful memories adorn our way,
Moments like sunbeams in bright array.
Through storms and trials, we stand strong,
In the tapestry, we belong.

Each stitch a story, each knot a time,
Binding our hearts in rhythm and rhyme.
With every encounter, we add a thread,
In the patterns of love, forever spread.

As seasons change, our colors blend,
In nature's embrace, there's no end.
For in this weave, we find our place,
Entwined in warmth, time can't erase.

A canvas alive, our tale unfurls,
In the threads of life, love whirls.
Together we paint, together we trust,
In this beautiful tapestry of us.

Echoes of Togetherness

In the quiet, our laughs resound,
Echoes of joy, a gentle sound.
Every heartbeat a shared refrain,
Together we dance through joy and pain.

Through tangled paths, we find our way,
With every step, we're here to stay.
Voices intertwined, a sweet embrace,
In every moment, we find our place.

With whispered secrets beneath the stars,
We ignite our dreams, no matter how far.
In echoes of togetherness we believe,
In the light of love, our hearts achieve.

Through shadows cast, we stand united,
In every challenge, our strength ignited.
With each sunrise, our spirits soar,
For in this bond, we find much more.

In every heartbeat, a song we share,
The melody of life, beyond compare.
Hand in hand, through thick and thin,
In echoes of togetherness, we begin.

Reaching Across Spaces

In the silence of night, I reach for you,
Through the distances, vast and blue.
With every heartbeat, a bridge we lay,
Reaching across, come what may.

Stars are our guide, lighting the way,
In the dreams we share, night turns to day.
Your laugh's a beacon, warm and bright,
Drawing me closer, a beautiful sight.

In every whisper, a promise made,
As time and space gently fade.
Through miles apart, our souls entwine,
In the tapestry of love, we shine.

Every tear, every joy, a thread we weave,
In this journey together, we believe.
No mountain too high, no river too wide,
With love as our compass, we will abide.

Reaching for dreams, both near and far,
Finding our light, no matter the scar.
In the vastness, love will suffice,
Reaching across spaces, we pay the price.

Affinities in the Shadows

In quiet corners, secrets lie,
Affinities born, unseen by the eye.
With whispered feels in twilight's grace,
We find our strength in a sacred space.

Underneath the stars, our hearts align,
In the whispers of night, we intertwine.
With every shadow, a story to tell,
In the depths of silence, we dwell.

Words unspoken, yet loudly felt,
In the shadowed warmth, our souls melt.
Embracing the dark, we learn to see,
Affinities bloom, wild and free.

In the dance of shadows, we create,
A world of wonders, born of fate.
Though hidden from light, our love shines bright,
Guiding us through the darkest night.

So let us linger in this twilight glow,
In the affinities shared, we grow.
For in the shadows, hand in hand,
We craft a meaning, timeless and grand.

A World Without Walls

In a land where horizons blend,
Dreams and hopes never end.
Voices travel on gentle breeze,
Uniting hearts with such ease.

Mountains bow to the sky,
Rivers hug the earth nearby.
No boundaries to divide the soul,
Together we can be whole.

We dance in the open air,
With laughter that we willingly share.
Hand in hand, we rise and fall,
In a world that knows no walls.

Each star shines in the night,
Guiding us with its light.
With every step, we learn to trust,
Together, it's a must.

A tapestry of colors bright,
Weaving stories in the light.
In unity, we find our call,
In a world, we build, without walls.

Sails of Togetherness

On a boat with sails so wide,
We navigate the rising tide.
With hearts as our compass, we'll steer,
Together, we'll conquer our fear.

Each wave carries dreams anew,
A journey meant for me and you.
The wind whispers sweet tales to tell,
Binding us in this shared spell.

Navigating through calm and storm,
In each embrace, our spirits warm.
We'll hoist our sails and chart our way,
Guided by love, come what may.

When clouds gather and skies turn gray,
Our sails will still find light of day.
In unity, we'll chart the course,
Together we feel love's force.

As horizons stretch beyond our sight,
Each journey brings new delight.
With sails unfurled, hearts in sync,
Together, we will never sink.

The Spirit of Connectivity

A thread that ties us, strong and fine,
Binding souls through space and time.
In every smile, in every glance,
We find the magic of our dance.

Like stars that twinkle in the night,
Our spirits gleam, a shared light.
Each whisper bridges far apart,
Connecting every beating heart.

Through laughter, tears, we weave our tale,
In every storm, we will not fail.
Together, we hold the key,
Unlock the doors to harmony.

The universe hums a sweet refrain,
In the quiet, we'll break the chain.
With open arms, we rise and stand,
Together, united, hand in hand.

In the tapestry of life we share,
A spirit binding everywhere.
In every moment, we revive,
The spirit of connectivity keeps us alive.

Echoing Hearts

In valleys deep where silence reigns,
An echo whispers through the plains.
It carries tales of love and dreams,
Uniting us in moonlit beams.

Each heartbeat resonates so clear,
A symphony for all to hear.
In every note, our stories blend,
In echoes, hearts begin to mend.

With every rise and every fall,
Our voices rise, we hear the call.
In unity, we find our way,
Echoing the songs we play.

The mountains cradle the sound so true,
As we sing, our spirits renew.
From dusk till dawn, let hearts ignite,
In echoes, we shine so bright.

Together we write, hand in heart,
The lyrics of life, each plays a part.
In resonance, love never departs,
Our lives entwined, echoing hearts.

Laughter in Distant Echoes

In twilight's embrace, we gather near,
With whispers of laughter, we shed our fear.
Echoes of joy dance on the breeze,
Carried by memories, they put us at ease.

Stars twinkle softly in the night sky,
As we share our stories, let time fly by.
Beneath the moon's glow, we feel so alive,
In this vibrant moment, our spirits thrive.

Old tales resurface, like waves on the shore,
Binding our hearts, we cherish them more.
Through laughter and dreams, we find our way,
In distant echoes, our souls can play.

Time may part us, like clouds in the blue,
But laughter remains, a thread that is true.
In every heartbeat, in every sigh,
Distant echoes linger, never saying goodbye.

So let us rejoice in the bonds we create,
In the dance of our laughter, it's never too late.
For in every chuckle, a promise we make,
That joy will connect us, no matter the fate.

Threads of Connection

In the tapestry of life, we weave so tight,
Each thread a story, a spark of light.
Through laughter and tears, our journeys blend,
Creating a fabric that will never end.

In crowded rooms, our eyes will meet,
A silent bond, a familiar beat.
Through gestures and smiles, we understand,
The unspoken ties that always stand.

Across vast distances, we reach with our hearts,
In moments of silence, our love imparts.
Each connection cherished, in time may grow,
Like rivers converging, they ebb and flow.

The beauty of friendships, a colorful thread,
Stitched with compassion, where dreams are spread.
In every heartbeat, a rhythm we share,
Threads of connection, woven with care.

So celebrate each bond, unique and bright,
In the loom of existence, we are the light.
With threads interlaced, our spirits entwine,
Together we flourish, our souls align.

Hearts Unveiled in Silence

In moments of stillness, our hearts are revealed,
With whispers of truth that remain unsealed.
In quiet reflection, we find our own way,
As silence speaks volumes, more than words say.

Eyes hold the stories we've yet to share,
In the depths of our souls, we silently care.
Through fleeting glances, connections ignite,
Hearts unveiled softly, in the cloak of night.

Beneath the surface, where emotions reside,
In the calm of the moment, our fears set aside.
A bond that transcends, no need for sound,
In the silence of trust, our hopes are found.

As stars bear witness to the secrets we keep,
With courage, we tread in this silence deep.
Embracing the stillness, we feel the embrace,
In hearts unveiled, we reclaim our space.

So let the silence speak, let it guide our way,
In the sanctuary of peace, we choose to stay.
Through whispers of love in the quiet we find,
That hearts unveiled blossom, forever intertwined.

Bridges of Understanding

Between us rise bridges, sturdy and tall,
Built from compassion, connecting us all.
In shared experiences, we lay the stone,
With empathy guiding, we're never alone.

Each step we take, we lightly tread,
Honoring paths where our fears have led.
Through laughter and sorrow, we navigate wide,
Bridges of understanding, hearts open wide.

In moments of doubt, we find our way back,
A journey together, we'll never lack.
Through dialogue gentle, our minds will engage,
Bridges of understanding, written on page.

With arms reaching out, we embrace the unknown,
In the warmth of our trust, seeds of hope are sown.
The strength of our unity, an unshakeable bond,
With bridges of understanding, we dream and respond.

So let's build a future with kindness at heart,
With hands intertwined, we'll never depart.
Through bridges we traverse, horizons expand,
In unity's glow, we forever will stand.

Where Strangers Meet

In the twilight hour, paths entwine,
Eyes meet in silence, stories align.
Whispers of hope in the evening air,
Two souls connect, each one laid bare.

Hands shake firmly, barriers fall,
A smile shared, uniting us all.
Differences fade, a bridge is made,
In the heart of the night, fears start to jade.

With each laugh, a bond is formed,
In this moment, we feel transformed.
Strangers once, now friends we'll be,
In the tapestry of life, you and me.

The sunset glows, its colors blend,
As time stops short, we comprehend.
From different worlds, yet here we stand,
Hand in hand, a shared strand.

So let us gather for just this night,
In the warmth of the fading light.
For where strangers meet, love is born,
In this precious moment, hearts are adorned.

Kinship Across Cultures

In every corner of the earth we roam,
Different languages, yet feelings close to home.
A nod, a gesture, a smile so wide,
In the dance of culture, we recognize pride.

From mountains high to oceans deep,
In tales shared, our hearts we keep.
Traditions cherished, passed down with care,
In kinship's embrace, we find what we share.

The feast is rich with flavors galore,
In laughter and song, we long for more.
A symphony of voices, a tapestry bright,
Together we rise, in love's pure light.

Differences fade when the music starts,
We learn through rhythm, and open our hearts.
Unity blooms, a flower in the sun,
In kinship across cultures, we become one.

As stars twinkle high in the infinite night,
We celebrate life, its beauty and light.
Together we stand, hand in hand,
In this world of colors, truly grand.

Merging Echoes

In the stillness, whispers converge,
Voices entwining, a gentle surge.
From silences shared, a harmony sings,
Merging echoes, the joy it brings.

Through laughter and tears, our stories collide,
In the heart of the moment, we take pride.
With every echo, a lifetime unfolds,
In tales of strength and dreams retold.

As rivers flow and mountains stand tall,
We find connections that bind us all.
Each note a thread in the tapestry,
Merging together, you and me.

In shadows cast by the setting sun,
We gather as one, the journey begun.
No longer alone on this winding road,
In merging echoes, our spirits explode.

So listen closely, let your heart feel,
In every echo, love's gentle wheel.
Together we rise, in unity's sway,
Merging echoes, lighting the way.

The Pulse of Togetherness

In the rhythm of life, can you hear it beat?
A pulse of togetherness that feels so sweet.
Hand in hand, we dance through the night,
Energized by love, our spirits take flight.

With every heartbeat, a story is told,
In layers of warmth, our hands we hold.
United in laughter, in sorrow, in grace,
The pulse of togetherness, a shared embrace.

Across the distances, our hearts remain true,
In the tapestry woven, it's me and it's you.
Every heartbeat echoes, every breath shared,
In this life's journey, we've all truly dared.

Through trials and triumphs, we learn and we grow,
The pulse of our bond, a river that flows.
In moments of silence, in raucous cheer,
Together we thrive, with nothing to fear.

So let us celebrate, the joy of our kin,
In the dance of togetherness, let life begin.
With hearts intertwined, we're never alone,
In the pulse of togetherness, we have found home.

The Dance of Diversity

In colors bright, we find our way,
Different beats in soft ballet.
Together swaying, hand in hand,
A vibrant tale across the land.

With every step, our stories blend,
New rhythms form, as hearts transcend.
Echoes of laughter fill the air,
A symphony of love laid bare.

No single path, no single song,
In unity, we all belong.
Each voice a thread, in life's grand weave,
A tapestry we all believe.

In twilight's glow, the dance persists,
Each twist and turn, impossible to resist.
Together we move, side by side,
In the dance of diversity, we take pride.

So let us move, let spirits rise,
In joyful harmony, we energize.
With open hearts, we break the chain,
In this dance of life, there's no disdain.

Souls on Common Ground

In quiet spaces, we can meet,
Hearts aligned, our rhythms beat.
With gentle smiles, we share our dreams,
A world much brighter than it seems.

Kindred spirits, side by side,
Across the shores, our hopes collide.
In each soft word, a bridge is laid,
A bond unspoken, yet conveyed.

As seasons change, we stand our ground,
In every trial, together found.
Through storms that rage, we remain strong,
In this shared journey, we belong.

United voices, sweet and clear,
Our laughter echoes, drawing near.
In every struggle, joy will sprout,
Souls on common ground, no doubt.

So take my hand, let's walk this way,
Together facing each new day.
In unity, our hearts will sing,
With love, all barriers we'll bring.

Embracing the Unknown

Beneath the stars, we take a chance,
With beating hearts, we start to dance.
The road ahead is shrouded, grey,
Yet hope ignites, it lights our way.

In whispered dreams, we dare to soar,
Through fog and doubt, we seek for more.
Adventure's call is loud and clear,
With open minds, we shed our fear.

Each step we take, a path unfolds,
In brave embrace, the future holds.
With every breath, we push the line,
Towards the horizon, we will shine.

In uncharted realms, we find our place,
With courage stitched into our grace.
Together we'll carve a brand new way,
Embracing the unknown, come what may.

Our spirits rise, a daring flight,
Through darkness deep, we search for light.
In the unknown, our souls ignite,
With every heartbeat, bold and bright.

Ties in the Twilight

As day retreats, the dusk arrives,
In shadows soft, our connection thrives.
With whispered words, our hearts align,
In the twilight glow, stars intertwine.

With every glance, a story shared,
In silences, our souls declared.
The world may fade, but we are near,
In this gentle twilight, there's no fear.

Threads of the past weave through our hearts,
In every ending, a new start.
Together we move, through dusk and dawn,
In timeless bonds, forever drawn.

As shadows lengthen, love draws close,
In quiet moments, the heart knows most.
Through changing skies, our journey flows,
With ties in twilight, love only grows.

So let the night embrace our dreams,
In silver light, we're more than beams.
For in this twilight, hand in hand,
A sacred bond will ever stand.

Coming Together in Quiet

In the hush of night we meet,
A gentle breeze, soft and sweet.
Whispers dance like falling leaves,
In this calm where time believes.

Hands touch lightly, hearts align,
Silent vows that intertwine.
Stars above begin to glow,
In the stillness, love will grow.

Moments drift like clouds in flight,
Wrapped in warmth, we share the light.
In this peace, we find our way,
A tender bond that's here to stay.

Words unspoken, eyes that speak,
In the quiet, strong and meek.
What is fleeting feels so vast,
In this moment, we are cast.

Together we can face the dawn,
With every shadow gently drawn.
Side by side, we rise anew,
In the quiet, me and you.

The Unseen Embrace

Beyond the noise, the world is still,
A quiet touch, it gives a thrill.
Invisible threads weave us tight,
In shadows cast by silver light.

The heart can sense what eyes can't see,
A silent bond, you and me.
In every heartbeat, every sigh,
An unseen hug that won't say goodbye.

Like gentle waves that kiss the shore,
Together we will always soar.
Through moments lost, through time we glide,
In every breath, we feel the tide.

The world may shift, but still we stand,
In unseen warmth, hand in hand.
No distance vast, no path too long,
In quiet love, we both belong.

Every heartbeat, every glance,
In the shadows, we will dance.
With strength unseen, we hold our place,
In every moment, an unseen embrace.

Unsung Harmonies

In the silence, notes collide,
Melodies where dreams reside.
Whispers hum, a gentle tune,
A chorus sung beneath the moon.

With every breath, we share this sound,
In the quiet, joy is found.
A symphony that knows no name,
In this harmony, we're the same.

Echoes linger as we sway,
In this dance, we find our way.
Voices blend in soft embrace,
A sweet refrain time won't erase.

Though unsung, our hearts unite,
Creating magic in the night.
In every moment, every start,
We write the song within our heart.

The world may not know our score,
But in this tune, we're evermore.
Together, we'll find our song to sing,
In unsung harmonies, our hearts take wing.

Finding Light in Shadows

In twilight's grasp, we search for rays,
Where light and dark twist in a maze.
Shadows whisper secrets deep,
In their arms, dreams softly sleep.

The sun may hide, but hope won't fade,
In every doubt, new plans are laid.
With every step in stillness found,
We learn that joy is all around.

Through cracks of light, we hear the call,
In every shadow, fears will fall.
A journey held, both stark and bright,
In every challenge, sparks ignite.

When heavy hearts refuse to soar,
We seek the warmth, we find the door.
In shadowed corners, love comes near,
Finding light in all we fear.

So let us walk through night and day,
In every gloom, there's hope to sway.
Together we'll embrace the change,
In finding light, we grow, we range.

Dance of Divergence

In the twilight's gentle sway,
Two paths diverge, a dance begins.
One whispers soft, the other shouts,
Each step a choice, as time spins thin.

Leaves flutter in the evening breeze,
Joyful echoes of laughter shared.
Yet in the silence, hearts can freeze,
A moment lost, dreams laid bare.

Together they twine, then drift apart,
As waves break on the shore of fate.
A symphony penned by each heart,
In melodies that resonate.

Footsteps mark a trail unseen,
Curved paths often lead to chance.
Through tangled woods where thoughts convene,
We find our names in evening's dance.

In this ballet, no end in sight,
A story told, both bold and meek.
As stars awaken in the night,
Our paths converge, yet never speak.

Fences Made of Flowers

A garden blooms, where colors blend,
Petals whisper secrets shared.
Fences made of blossoms bend,
Each fragrant promise laid and dared.

Vines twine softly, reach and clasp,
Holding dreams in their tender grasp.
In the sunlit hours, stories bask,
Nature's art within a simple task.

Butterflies flit on gentle wings,
Dancing on the cusp of spring.
From thorn to bloom, the heart still sings,
In the beauty that each season brings.

A symphony of colors bright,
Painting shadows on the ground.
With every morn, new dreams take flight,
In a world where love is found.

Between the blooms, we build our space,
Where laughter sways and sorrows cease.
In this haven, find your place,
Fences made of flowers, peace.

The Art of Listening

In the stillness where words fade,
Silence holds a deeper sound.
The heart in quietude is laid,
In gentle ways, the truth is found.

A whisper glimmers in the dark,
Soft echoes through the weight of night.
In shadows, sparks ignite a spark,
Emotions dance in fragile light.

Eyes meet softly, stories flow,
Every glance a canvas drawn.
In the spaces where feelings grow,
The art of listening is reborn.

Underneath the noise and haste,
Lies a realm where souls convene.
Each heartbeat offers time and space,
To understand what lies unseen.

So open wide your heart and mind,
Let stillness cradle every sigh.
In silence, we are intertwined,
The art of listening, our reply.

When Shadows Meet Light

In the merging of day and night,
Where shadows stretch and secrets hide.
Softly whispered dreams take flight,
As the sun and moon collide.

In twilight's glow, colors blend,
Darkness meets with radiant beams.
With every twist, a journey bends,
In these moments, we find dreams.

Underneath the fading sky,
Ghostly figures dance and sway.
With each heartbeat, soft goodbyes,
And promises held in the gray.

Reflections murmur in the dark,
Where wonders fade in twilight's hue.
In the silence, we leave a mark,
Illuminated by all we knew.

When shadows meet the briefest light,
The world becomes a canvas bright.
In that space, we find our fight,
In the darkness, we find our sight.

Celebrating the Unique

In every shade, a story blooms,
Voices rise, dispelling glooms.
Colors dance in vibrant cheer,
Embracing all that we hold dear.

Each quirk is like a starry night,
Flashes of joy, a dazzling sight.
Together we form a wondrous blend,
A tapestry that will not end.

Through laughter shared and tears we shed,
In every heart, a thread is said.
We are the music, rich and true,
An anthem sung in every hue.

So let us raise our voices high,
In unity, we will not shy.
Embrace the unique, let love ignite,
In every soul, a shining light.

We stand as one, with arms out wide,
Celebrating all, in love, we bide.
A world made brighter by our touch,
In every heart, we share so much.

The Heart's Compass

When shadows fall and roads seem dark,
The heart will guide, it leaves a mark.
In whispers soft, it knows the way,
Through stormy nights to break of day.

It beats with hope, a silent song,
Reminding us where we belong.
Through trials faced, it won't unwind,
A loyal friend, its love is blind.

Each dream we chase, each path we choose,
The heart reveals what we might lose.
In every flutter, it holds the key,
Unlocking doors to what can be.

Though fears may creep and doubt may rise,
The heart reflects the brightest skies.
In moments still, it shows the truth,
A steadfast guide in tender youth.

So trust its call and let it lead,
For in its dance, we will succeed.
In every beat, a chance to soar,
The heart's compass opens every door.

Paths Intertwined

Two strangers walking, fates collide,
A journey shared, hearts open wide.
With every step, our stories merge,
In a new dance, we find our urge.

As seasons change, together we grow,
Learning from each other, soft and slow.
In laughter's echo and tears we share,
We weave our paths with tender care.

Through tangled roots and branches high,
Our lives entwined like the endless sky.
In moments fleeting and those that last,
We cherish the future while honoring the past.

Each twist and turn is a lesson learned,
With every victory, a heart that's burned.
Yet through the trials, we find a way,
In every ending, there's a new day.

So let us walk with hands held tight,
In the tapestry of day and night.
Together we'll shine, our spirits aligned,
In the beautiful dance of paths intertwined.

Where Dissonance Meets

In discord's shadow, silence breathes,
Yet often truth is what it leaves.
Amidst the noise, we search for peace,
A moment where our worries cease.

Through chaos formed, new patterns rise,
In shattered notes, we hear the sighs.
For every clash, a harmony waits,
Creating beauty from the fates.

Unruly hearts, together we stand,
Connecting fragments, hand in hand.
In every struggle, we find our way,
Dissonance guides the light of day.

So let the tension fill the air,
For in the clash, there's love to share.
In every note, both sharp and sweet,
Lies the dance where opposites meet.

In this embrace of dark and light,
We find our strength in the fight.
In every discord, a vibrant song,
Where dissonance meets, we belong.

Unseen Bridges

Between each heart, a bridge is laid,
Invisible paths, in silence made.
Together we walk, though apart we stand,
A connection so deep, it's hard to understand.

In whispered thoughts, we share our dreams,
Through cosmic threads, or so it seems.
With every step on this silent way,
The bridges we build will never fray.

Time may stretch, and distance grow,
Yet love's soft light will always glow.
We reach across, though miles divide,
In unseen bridges, we will confide.

Each heartbeat binds, with threads of gold,
Stories of warmth in the winter cold.
Through laughter's echoes, through tear-streaked eyes,
Unseen, unbroken, our spirit flies.

So cherish the bridges that join our souls,
In every silence, in every scroll.
For though we're apart, we're never far,
In the tapestry spun, you're my guiding star.

Hearts in Harmony

Two voices rise, a gentle song,
In harmony, where we belong.
Each note we share, a perfect blend,
In symphonies that never end.

We dance through life, each step a rhyme,
In cherished moments, lost in time.
With every heartbeat, we sing as one,
Together we shine, like the morning sun.

In all our trials, in joy and strife,
Our hearts entwined, the rhythm of life.
Side by side, we stand so strong,
In the melody, we both belong.

From whispered winds to thunder's call,
In every rise, in every fall.
We find our pulse in nature's tune,
Beneath the stars, under the moon.

In soft reflections, our love is clear,
In hearts in harmony, with nothing to fear.
Together we sing, through thick and thin,
With every melody, our souls begin.

Ties that Transcend

In moments shared, our ties are spun,
Stronger than time, and never done.
A thread of fate in every glance,
In this great dance, we take a chance.

Through storms we weather, side by side,
In laughter's glow, we take our stride.
These bonds are forged in the fires of truth,
Rooted in wisdom, encased in youth.

Even in silence, we understand,
The touch of a heart, a gentle hand.
In every struggle, in every cheer,
These ties that transcend, we hold dear.

From memories bright to shadows cast,
Each moment cherished, each heartbeat fast.
In life's vast tapestry, we are sewn,
In the garden of kinship, love has grown.

Through changing seasons, we will remain,
In ties that transcend, with joy and pain.
Together we'll rise, together we'll bend,
In the circle of life, as lovers and friends.

The Language of Souls

In a glance exchanged, worlds collide,
No words are spoken, yet love won't hide.
Through whispered sighs and laughter's tune,
We find our meaning beneath the moon.

Each heartbeat echoes, a story told,
In the language of souls, we're brave and bold.
With every touch, with every sigh,
In silent moments, we learn to fly.

The universe speaks, in colors and light,
In each gentle breeze, in day and night.
We dance on the edge of time and space,
In this cosmic bond, we find our place.

Through trials faced, together we stand,
In the language of souls, we understand.
With every heartbeat, together we grow,
In the garden of life, love's seeds we sow.

So listen closely, when silence speaks,
In the language of souls, it's love that peaks.
With hearts wide open, and spirits free,
We'll write our story, just you and me.

Unity in Diversity

In many colors, we stand tall,
Voices mingle, answering the call.
Different paths, yet one bright sky,
Together we reach, together we fly.

Each story unique, like a star's light,
Shining together in the night.
Hand in hand, we break the mold,
In unity's grasp, brave and bold.

Cultures blend, a vibrant hue,
Learning from me, and learning from you.
A garden rich, in every bloom,
Let love flourish, dispersing gloom.

Harmony whispers, in every heart,
Joining forces, we'll never part.
In every difference, a chance to grow,
Together, we rise, together we glow.

So here we gather, strong and free,
Embracing all, in unity.
For in our hearts, the truth we find,
A tapestry of the human mind.

Embracing Differences

In every face, a story lies,
Rich experiences, open skies.
With arms wide open, we invite,
The beauty of differences shines so bright.

Let's celebrate, no need to hide,
Celebrate each other, side by side.
Every voice matters, every song,
Together in harmony, we belong.

The strength we find in what divides,
Builds our bridges, where love abides.
In the dance of life, we sway and twirl,
Sharing our hearts, we change the world.

With laughter shared and kindness spread,
We weave a thread where hope is bred.
In shadows cast, we see the light,
Embracing differences, shining bright.

So let us gather in joyous cheer,
Embrace each other, hold us near.
In every heartbeat, a chance to see,
The magic found in you and me.

Through the Walls

Walls may rise, but hearts can break,
With gentle whispers, we awake.
Beyond the barriers, patience grows,
In understanding, love bestows.

Listen closely, to the silent cries,
See through the surface, where the truth lies.
In every corner, a hidden space,
A shared connection, a warm embrace.

Through thick and thin, we reach and strive,
Hope is the force that keeps us alive.
Breaking down walls, we gather near,
Creating a world where love is clear.

With each step forward, we take the lead,
Transforming hearts, planting the seed.
In our differences, we find the thread,
Of unity's promise, where paths are led.

So let us venture, hand in hand,
Through the walls that once made us stand.
In this journey, together we'll see,
A brighter tomorrow, for you and for me.

Threads of Empathy

Each thread we weave tells a tale,
Of laughter shared, or times we pale.
In every fiber, a story flows,
Connecting our hearts, as friendship grows.

Empathy binds us in gentle grace,
In understanding, we find our place.
A tender touch can heal the pain,
In woven threads, love can remain.

When silence speaks, we learn to hear,
The unvoiced sorrows, the hidden fear.
With open arms, we stand as one,
Underneath the same shining sun.

In the tapestry of life so grand,
Threads of kindness, each made by hand.
Through storms we weather, together we find,
A tapestry rich, through heart and mind.

So let us cherish each thread we hold,
Crafting our stories, brave and bold.
In the fabric of life, let's intertwine,
Threads of empathy, forever divine.